I HATE PRINCETON
303 Reasons Why You Should, Too

Crane Hill
PUBLISHERS
BIRMINGHAM, ALABAMA
1996

I HATE PRINCETON
303 Reasons Why You Should, Too

by Paul Finebaum

CRANE HILL
PUBLISHERS

Copyright 1996 by Paul Finebaum

All rights reserved
Printed in the United States of America
Published by Crane Hill Publishers
Many thanks to John Carrigan.

Library of Congress Cataloging-in-Publication Data

Finebaum, Paul, 1955-
   I hate Princeton: 303 reasons why you should, too / Paul Finebaum.
     p.   cm.
   ISBN 1-57587-007-X
   1. Princeton University -- Football -- Miscellanea.   I. Title.
GV958.P7F55   1996
796.332'64'0974965--dc20   96-7053
                                                                                                    CIP

10   9   8   7   6   5   4   3   2   1

I HATE PRINCETON

I Hate Princeton Because…

1. Coach Pete Carril once said, "Winning a national championship is not something you're going to do at Princeton. I resigned myself to that years ago."

2. President Bill Clinton's commencement speech at Princeton was titled "Women, Booze, and Drugs: Now You See Why I Went to Yale."

3. President Clinton agreed to speak at Princeton in exchange for a year's supply of footlong chili dogs from Varsity Deli.

4. After 8 consecutive wins, it took a 10-10 tie with Dartmouth for Princeton to be declared the "Outright Ivy Champs" in 1995.

5. Coach Steve Tosches once said, "You can tell a Princeton coed is really good in bed when she loses her place in a book more than once."

6. Princeton has put 3 presidents in the Oval Office, but they can't put 1 basketball team past Penn.

7. When talking about his coaching career at Princeton, Pete Carril usually says, "I think I'll have a nice talk with God and ask Him, 'Why did You do this to me?'"

8. Bill Clinton was overheard telling Princeton grad Steve Forbes, "The Flat Tax was my idea. Hillary thought up the No Tax."

9. Steve Forbes is working on a book about his presidential candidacy titled *If You Can't Win After Spending 33 Million Bucks, You Must Suck.*

10. If Steve Forbes had won, he would have been the first American president to have repeated the eighth grade.

11. Princeton couldn't win the championship even when Dean Cain, TV's Superman, was on the team.

12. The top 10 most popular phrases overheard on Princeton's campus are: "Who has the clapper this time?"

13. "Which dorm room was Dean Cain's?"

14. "So, did Penn beat us again last night?"

15. "Well, there's always next year."

16. "I know it's called The Beach, but where's the water?"

17. "Don't walk out the FitzRandolph Gate."

18. "Will Andre be coming to the reunion with Brooke Shields?"

19. "Brooke who?"

20. "Have you heard about the brain story?"

21. "Where can we buy a cheap clapper?"

22. John F. Kennedy went to Princeton, but for only a year—he left when he found out most of the coeds were virgins.

23. Princeton is the only school in the Ivy League where the women have facial hair and the men have PMS.

24. Pete Carril's top 10 excuses for not winning the NCAA tournament are: White men can't jump.

25. Brawn wins over brains every time.

26. The other schools cheat.

27. There aren't enough good-looking women at Princeton to attract top-flight players.

28. Princeton's campus sucks.

29. Jadwin Gym is a joke.

30. The administration cares more about winning Nobel prizes than going to the Final Four.

31. President Harold T. Shapiro is a closet John Thompson fan.

32. Princeton players are afraid of black people.

33. God doesn't want me to win.

34. Every time he loses a game, coach Pete Carril says, "I'll take this up with God when I get there."

35. Winnie Holzman based her acclaimed TV series *My So-Called Life* on her experiences at Princeton.

36. Alan Blinder returned to campus recently from the Federal Reserve Board because he got tired of Alice Rivlin trying to hit on him.

37. President Harold T. Shapiro likes to brag that he's related to Robert Shapiro.

38. A recent poll of students revealed that the 10 biggest geeks to ever attend Princeton are: Steve Forbes.

39. Bill Bradley.

40. William Paterson.

41. Woodrow Wilson.

42. Elias Boudinot.

43. Harold T. Shapiro.

44. Aaron Lemonick.

45. Gary Walters.

46. Dave Calone.

47. James Madison.

48. Princeton freshmen think Firestone Library is where they're supposed to go to buy new tires.

49. After his freshman year John F. Kennedy left due to illness–he was sick of Princeton.

50. Before football coach Steve Tosches is allowed to teach a course at Princeton, he should be required to pass one.

51. Banning David Cordish from Princeton tennis matches was the best thing the NCAA ever did.

52. "Money talks" doesn't apply to Steve Forbes's money.

53. Gary Walters is to athletics what the *Titanic* was to luxury cruise ships.

54. The top 10 pickup lines recently overheard on Princeton's campus are: "I'm Dean Cain's brother."

55. "I taught Pete Carril how to dribble."

56. "Nice buns."

57. "Oh, I'm sorry. I thought you were governor Christine Whitman."

58. "Hello, I'm James Madison XV."

59. "I took the clapper from the bell tower. Want to see it?"

60. "Do you happen to know where Netscape closed today?"

61. "Did I mention that I'm a Kennedy?"

62. "And I'm loaded."

63. "Hi. I'm Pete Carril. I have lots of spare time now."

64. When the AP took a picture of coach Steve Tosches and Heisman contender Dave Patterson, they wanted it to look natural—so they posed Patterson with his hand in Tosches's pocket.

65. Coach Pete Carril said that sportswriter Paul Finebaum reminded him of Moses. Finebaum thought it was a compliment until Carril added, "Yeah, every time he opens his mouth the bull rushes."

66. Coach Bill Carmody thinks the movie *The Return of the Jedi* was based on the Tigers returning to Jadwin Gym after a road trip.

67. Princeton is the fourth oldest college in the country–and the dorms smell like it.

68. Coach Pete Carril has written a book titled *The 20 Biggest NCAA Games I've Choked In.*

69. President Harold T. Shapiro once started a speech by saying, "What do you get when you cross a Latter-day Saint and a hit of LSD? A high priest."

70. Coach Carril is so old that he recently bought tenderizer for his cornflakes.

71. Princeton's 1996 football schedule includes: Haverford (Away).

72. Martha Stewart's Cooking School (Home).

73. Radcliffe (Away).

74. Juilliard (Home).

75. Johns Hopkins (Away).

76. Ted Kennedy's School of Driving (Home).

77. Bennington (Away).

78. Smith (Home).

79. Vassar (Away).

80. Marlin Perkins's School of Obedience (Home).

81. Pete Carril's next job will most likely require a hair net.

82. The Princeton cheerleaders have income tax figures, and they should be arrested for not filling out their forms.

83. Sportscaster Tom McCarthy's brain has paused permanently for station identification.

84. Athletic director Gary Walters must get up early every morning–how else can he say so many stupid things in a day?

85. Elias Boudinot once said, "Never put off until tomorrow what you can do the day after tomorrow."

86. The most exciting part of a game at Palmer Stadium is the laser show at halftime.

87. Coach Pete Carril learned his court manners from Dennis Rodman.

88. Paul Finebaum's column is required reading for all Princeton players. Audiotapes are provided for those who can't read.

89. President Harold T. Shapiro is so unpopular that his therapist sends him hate mail.

90. President Shapiro is famous for saying, "You can tell your wife is ugly when a cannibal takes one look at her and orders a salad."

91. If sportscaster Tom McCarthy died during a game, no one would notice.

92. Most Princeton fans believe the Tiger should be given a high dose of Ritalin and sent home.

93. Palmer Stadium would make a nice nuclear test site.

94. Princeton's colors are black and orange, but during football season they are predominantly black and blue.

95. The average ACT score for incoming Princeton coeds is 29, which is also the number of their sex partners.

96. The top 10 most practical uses for the *The Daily Princetonian* are: Toilet paper.

97. Birdcage liner.

98. Fire starter.

99. Fly swatter.

100. A fine example of how *not* to write.

101. A wonderful gift for someone you hate.

102. An effective insect repellent.

103. Folded correctly it makes a great party hat.

104. An informative place mat, complete with pictures.

105. A substitute for the daily newspaper comics.

106. Coach Pete Carril is fond of complaining that nature is indifferent to the plight of man.

107. President Harold T. Shapiro's recent speech to the faculty was up to his usual substandard.

108. Last New Year's Eve president Harold T. Shapiro proposed this toast: "Here's to our wives and our sweethearts—may the two never meet."

109. Many years ago president Shapiro said, "I'm going to have to marry a virgin because I can't stand criticism."

110. Coach Pete Carril is so boring that he makes Sabrina Forbes look like a Harley biker.

111. Coach Pete Carril once told Bill Bradley that he could make more money in the NBA than in the U.S. Senate.

112. President Harold T. Shapiro hates the sight of liquor. He drinks all he can just to get it out of sight.

113. Athletic director Gary Walters knew his marriage was in trouble when his wife started wearing a black armband on their anniversary.

114. President Harold T. Shapiro and his wife have a mutual relationship—he's the mute.

115. A Princeton diploma is redeemable for 1 free sloppy joe at Hoagie Haven.

116. Steve Forbes's top 10 favorite pastimes while at Princeton were: Watching the stock ticker at the local Smith Barney office.

117. Debating the value of the yen with foreign students.

118. Stealing *Fortune* magazines from the bookstore so nobody would buy them.

119. Arguing with economic professors over the Flat Tax.

120. Rubbing sandpaper on his face.

121. Bragging to other students about his father's money.

122. Running negative ads about professors who gave him bad grades.

123. Wearing "Steve Forbes for President" buttons.

124. Bragging to gym teachers that he weighed less than his wife.

125. Leading campus boycotts of Dole pineapple.

126. The Ivy League has banned women from playing for Princeton because the other schools complained it would give them an unfair advantage.

127. The Firestone Library holds one of the largest collections of books and egos in the world.

128. Princeton uniforms have 2 numbers on them: the player's number and the number following his last name.

129. President Harold T. Shapiro is a second-story man—nobody ever believes his first story.

130. The flags at Princeton fly at half-mast on Malcolm Forbes's birthday.

131. A freshman once asked a senior where he could find a good football game. The senior gave him directions to Ohio State.

132. President Harold T. Shapiro's wife recently said these Shakespearean lines remind her of her husband: "He is no less than a stuffed man."

133. "He is but a filthy piece of work."

134. "I abhor this dilatory sloth."

135. "He is the bluntest wooer in Christendom."

136. "I had rather be married to a death's head with a bone in his mouth."

137. "More of his conversation would infect my brain."

138. "He speaks an infinite deal of nothing."

139. "How fiery and forward our pedant is!"

140. "There's no more faith in him than in a stewed prune."

141. "He has not so much brain as earwax."

142. "Wake when some vile thing is near."

143. Princeton University contributes a lot to the town–if you count the town hookers and pushers.

144. *Grumpy Old Men* was loosely based on the life of coach Pete Carril.

145. When President Harold T. Shapiro was asked what Winnie the Pooh and John the Baptist had in common, he responded, "They have the same middle name."

146. When destitute Princeton students call the Suicide Hotline, trained volunteers are sent to help them jump.

147. Dave Patterson is so bad that his mother should have thrown him away and kept the stork.

148. Princeton's football program peaks in July.

149. The fans have nicknamed football player Brock Harvey "Judge" because he spends so much time on the bench.

150. Princeton has installed a Morning After hotline and a Website for students who think they might be pregnant. Too bad Malcolm Forbes, Sr., didn't use them.

151. Most Princeton students think the Betty Ford Clinic is a post-graduate program.

152. The top 10 personalized tags seen on Princeton's campus are: SNOB.

153. NUMONEY

154. FLATTAX.

155. IMARICHMN.

156. MNYMNYMNY.

157. DOWJONES.

158. 2RICH4U.

159. TRSTFND.

160. RICHBCH.

161. FRBE.

162. One Princeton undergraduate recently took an aptitude test—it showed he was best suited for retirement.

163. The quickest way to empty a room at the Princeton business school is to scream, "Steve Forbes has decided to run for president again."

164. At Princeton a sit-in is a good excuse for skipping class. It's also more exciting than any of the basketball or football games.

165. Hillary Rodham Clinton couldn't get into Princeton because her thighs were too small.

166. To meet the demands of students, the Princeton administration has agreed to add more ethnic studies to the curriculum. The first new course offered will be "How to Make a Buck in a Third World Country."

167. A follow-up course will be "Child Labor Laws: Are They Really Children?"

168. Coach Steve Tosches is disagreeable, stupid, repulsive, and obnoxious—and those are his good points.

169. The top 10 career goals of Princetonians are: To marry one of Steve Forbes's girls.

170. To be president of the World Bank.

171. To win the New Jersey Lottery.

172. To marry governor Christine Whitman if she ever dumps her dorky husband.

173. To marry one of Bill Bradley's kids.

174. To become one of Al Sharpton's law partners.

175. To successfully blackmail Steve Forbes.

176. To win the *Reader's Digest* sweepstakes.

177. To have a McDonald's server spill hot coffee on you.

178. To have O. J. Simpson attempt to kill you but not succeed.

179. During his year at Princeton, JFK became enraged when the Student Union wouldn't let him use Swiss francs to pay for his morning coffee and donuts.

180. Watching Princeton lacrosse games is about as exciting as watching the 1994 Major League baseball season.

181. A Princeton graduate said to his Penn neighbor, "Do you actually have any hope of being accepted into my exclusive club?" The neighbor replied, "Sure—they've got to have someone to snub."

182. A major misconception about the value of a Princeton diploma is that it will get the graduate a job outside the boroughs.

183. Princeton grad Steve Forbes is a good excuse for alternative medicine.

184. Coach Steve Tosches is an experiment in Artificial Stupidity.

185. If football player Dave Patterson were any slower, he'd be in reverse.

186. If president Harold T. Shapiro has the chance to live his life over again, he shouldn't do it.

187. *Emergency Contraception: The Nation's Best-Kept Secret* by James Trussell is a bestseller at Princeton.

188. The biggest adjustment for new Princeton graduates is having to wear flame-retardant uniforms to work.

189. Princeton football players like to play David & Goliath with their jockstraps.

190. President Harold T. Shapiro graduated magna cum loudest.

191. Coach Pete Carril starts every practice by yelling, "Yo Yo Yo Yo Yo!"

192. President Harold T. Shapiro once said, "I'd like to buy Steve Tosches for what he's worth and sell him for what he thinks he's worth."

193. If what you don't know can't hurt you, coach Steve Tosches is practically invulnerable.

194. Coach Tosches says, "There's no use worrying about life because you'll never get out of it alive."

195. William Bowen keeps his office obsessively clean because he doesn't want to bite the dust.

196. Coach Steve Tosches got a life once, but he wasn't sure what to do with it.

197. Princeton has started a javelin retrieval team.

198. Dave Patterson used to brag that one of his teachers called him a flathead. He told everyone that he didn't realize he was so levelheaded.

199. Coach Steve Tosches once said, "If lessons are to be learned in defeat, our team is getting a great education."

200. The median IQ at Princeton doubles every time the football team leaves town for a road game.

201. One former Princeton quarterback went to a psychiatrist because he was feeling suicidal. The shrink asked for payment in advance.

202. Tom McCarthy doesn't have enough brain cells for Prozac to be effective.

203. Princeton students think they're getting higher education when they have a class on the top floor of Jadwin Gym.

204. Some Princeton basketball players tried to enlist this year rather than wait for the NBA draft.

205. It's easy to be humble when you're a Princeton fan.

206. The Princeton English professors watch *Beavis and Butthead* to learn vocabulary.

207. The Princeton sociology professors require their students to watch TV sitcoms–it's the only way they'll learn about the middle class.

208. When JFK walked into his first class at Princeton, the teacher said, "Welcome to this class. A fool can ask questions that even wise men can't answer. That's why so many people fail this course."

209. Princeton's crack Sports Information Department staff is known as Winken, Blinken, and Nod.

210. Sportscaster Tom McCarthy says he often gets lost in thought. It's easy to get lost where one is a stranger.

211. President Harold T. Shapiro thinks that March Madness is something the psychology department should study.

212. Tiger football fans watch replays on Monday night hoping the score might change.

213. Coach Pete Carril thought the Final Four was the last call for drinks at a local Princeton bar.

214. Princeton students have to ask their parents about the last time the Tiger football team played in a bowl game.

215. Athletic director Gary Walters is first in line for a charisma transplant.

216. The Tiger has fleas.

217. Coach Steve Tosches attributes losing seasons to youth and injury. Fans attribute them to ignorant calls and an enormous ego.

218. The best place to stay in Princeton is out of town.

219. The best form of birth control for Princeton cocds is nudity.

220. The Princeton homecoming queen was recently taken to a dog show, and she won.

221. Coach Pete Carril keeps opening things by mistake–mostly his mouth.

222. The bestselling bumper sticker in the Princeton bookstore is "Wait Till Next Year."

223. The top 5 reasons students chose to attend the University of Princeton are: Harvard was full.

224. Yale's requirements were too stiff.

225. They wanted to attend a school that didn't have a nationally ranked football team.

226. Their parents didn't want them to be distracted by watching their football team play on national television.

227. They wanted to attend a school where they wouldn't have to wait in line for football tickets.

228. Jadwin Gym is a great place to watch a basketball game because there aren't any national championship banners to block the view.

229. William Bowen is the kind of guy who goes to an orgy and complains about the cheese dip.

230. What do Princeton students call their Yale counterparts after graduation? Boss.

231. The Tiger fans' favorite television station is QVC.

232. The fact that Palmer Stadium seats 57,800 just proves how little there is to do in Princeton.

233. Sportswriters Tom Canavan and Rich Fisher began their careers as reporters for *The National Enquirer.*

234. The captain of the Princeton cheerleading team was recently voted the most likely to conceive.

235. Before hiring a new coaching staff, Steve Tosches told athletic director Gary Walters, "Princeton doesn't need to get rid of the coaches. We just need to find a way to get rid of the alumni."

236. The only thing worse than a Tiger fan is 2 Tiger fans.

237. Coach Pete Carril's face looks better from the back.

238. Coach Steve Tosches is very creative–he makes a new mistake every day.

239. The only exercise athletic director Gary Walter gets is stretching the truth.

240. Princeton basketball fans have come to know the four seasons well: basketball, basketball recruiting, cheating, and more cheating.

241. Princeton doesn't have to worry about the NCAA's rule on NFL recruiting—no NFL recruits come to Princeton.

242. Pete Carril has been at Princeton so long that he and Woodrow Wilson used to double date.

243. President Harold T. Shapiro is always trying–trying people's patience.

244. If Princeton grad Steve Forbes sits down too hard, he gives himself a concussion.

245. Pete Carril secretly wants to coach at Harvard.

246. Princeton football has always been known for upholding tradition–a losing tradition.

247. *The Daily Princetonian* has an illustrated edition for athletes.

248. The Princeton basketball players top 5 favorite pastime activities are: Picking fights with coeds.

249. Picking fights with small children.

250. Trying to guess the last time the Princeton football team won a game.

251. Calling up the NCAA and screaming, "Penn cheats too!"

252. Calling up the NCAA and saying, "This is coach Al Bagnoli, and I want to turn myself in."

253. Most people live and learn—coach Steve Tosches just lives.

254. There is something to be said for coach Pete Carril, and he is usually saying it.

255. Pete Carril's favorite saying is "The past ain't what it used to be."

256. With Steve Tosches as head football coach, Princeton fans never have to worry about missing a basketball game because of a bowl game.

257. New York radio host Don Imus once told a cab driver, "Yes, I would like to see Howard Stern's private parts."

258. Coach Pete Carril can say less in more time than any other human being in the world.

259. Coach Carril is so old that his mind has gone from passion to pension.

260. If ignorance is bliss, sportscaster Tom McCarthy should be the happiest person in Princeton.

261. President Harold T. Shapiro once said that marriage is the only war in which you sleep with the enemy.

262. A Princeton athlete won a silver medal in the last Olympics. He was so proud that he had it bronzed.

263. Athletic director Gary Walters has a clear mind– that's because it's not cluttered with facts.

264. Coach Pete Carril refers to his players as "lightbulbs."

265. Sportscaster Ed Benkin once said, "The best thing about football is that it only takes four quarters to finish a fifth."

266. One Princeton basketball recruit got his red BMW the hard way—he bought it.

267. Steve Tosches's best coaching days are obviously in front of him.

268. Coach Tosches is as graceless in defeat as he is in victory.

269. Al Bagnoli's picture is on the wall of every post office in Princeton.

270. Princeton knew Dave Patterson would need lots of remedial help when they found out he couldn't spell "SAT."

271. Before Princeton grads receive their degrees, they must show proof of purchase slips for at least 2 textbooks.

272. Princeton may be New Jersey's oldest and largest university, but it's also the only one without a national championship in football.

273. A diploma from Princeton is about as valuable as Ronald McDonald's autograph.

274. Princeton cheerleaders don't like to lie out in the sun because the heat might melt their plastic surgery.

275. Princeton brags about its large number of Academic All-Americans, but all it means is that their jocks understand exactly why they are losers.

276. It's a misdemeanor for a Princeton player to snort the chalk lines on the practice field.

277. Princeton is the only town in America where the unemployment office has valet parking.

278. Basketball player Sydney Johnson once got a foul in an empty room.

279. One of the favorite field trips of Princeton football players is visiting Congress—especially when there's a joint session.

280. Basketball player Sydney Johnson once told an interviewer that he thought ACT stood for Athletes Cheat on Tests.

281. The Princeton student newspaper is the only one in America that lists the daily price of pot.

282. Athletic director Gary Walters never lets the facts interfere with his opinions.

283. The dean of Princeton's law school once said, "The worst thing about our trial system is that you leave your fate in the hands of 12 people too stupid to get out of jury duty."

284. Coach Pete Carril is writing a book called *All the Different Ways I've Blown the Penn Game*.

285. Dave Patterson once asked to change his major at Princeton because he thought physical education was just too hard.

286. *Playboy* featured the Tiger in its "Girls of the Ivy League" story because there were no good-looking Princeton coeds.

287. Coach Pete Carril's favorite fantasy is Penn shutting down its basketball program.

288. Sportscaster Ed Benkin once said, "I was born at night—but it wasn't last night."

289. If Princeton dropped their basketball program, would anybody notice?

290. The first-place prize in a recent radio giveaway was a pair of Princeton season football tickets. The second-place prize was 2 pairs of tickets.

291. A football player once sued sportscaster Tom McCarthy for calling him an "offensive lineman."

292. President Harold T. Shapiro doesn't like sex because you have to start at the top and work your way to the bottom.

293. As quarterbacks go, Dave Patterson is a fine broadcaster.

294. Currently there's an APB out for football player Brock Harvey's professional career.

295. As far as talk-show hosts go, Bob Grant would make a fine cab driver.

296. Princeton fans have a love-hate relationship with Al Bagnoli. They'd love for him to retire because they hate losing to him every year.

297. Sydney Johnson dribbles all over himself–but that doesn't make him a great basketball player.

298. Mike and the Mad Dog of WFAN are the best reasons to support the FCC.

299. There's no truth to the rumor that Princeton only gets the recruits Al Bagnoli doesn't want. The truth is that Princeton only gets the recruits *no* coach wants.

300. Len Berman of WNBC has only 2 faults: everything he does and everything he says.

301. Howard Stern placed an ad in *The Daily Princetonian* for heterosexual men and women to play extras in his upcoming movie–only 2 students responded.

302. New York radio host Don Imus is teaching a course at Princeton called "The Most Ignorant Things to Say During a White House Banquet."

303. The biggest seller at the campus bookstore this fall will be *I Hate Paul Finebaum* by Tommy Charles.